NELLO

The image on the Shroud

Results of photography and information technology

Translated by Alan Neame

ST PAULS

Series: THE SHROUD OF TURIN

1. Shroud, Gospels and Christian life.
2. The Shroud under the microscope. Forensic examination.
3. On the trail of the Shroud. Early and recent history.
4. An 'inexplicable' image. Theories on how the image on the Shroud was formed.
5. The image on the Shroud. Results of photography and information technology.
6. Shroud, carbon dating and calculus of probabilities.
7. Myrrh, aloes, pollen and other traces. Botanical research on the Shroud.

On the front cover: The three-dimensional Face on the Shroud, 'cleaned' of the marks of martyrdom (Photo N. Balossino – G. Tamburelli).
Photographs: N. Balossino, G. Tamburelli (2, 7, 8, 9, 10, 11, 12, 13, 14, 15, 17, 18, 19, 20, 21, 22); G. Enrie (1, 4, 5, 6); M. Moroni (16); S. Pia (3).

ST PAULS
Ireland
London SW1P 1EP, United Kingdom

© ST PAULS (UK) 1998

ISBN 085439 536 9

Set by TuKan, High Wycombe
Produced in the EC
Printed by The Guernsey Press Co. Ltd, Guernsey, C.I.

ST PAULS is an activity of the priests and brothers of the Society of St Paul who proclaim the Gospel through the media of social communication

CONTENTS

Bibliography	4
Photographic characteristics of the Shroud	6
Enhancement of the Shroud with information technology	12
Three-dimensionality	18
Detailed analysis of the three-dimensional image	24
The Shroud's natural face	28
Imprints of coins in the hollows of the eyes	32
The Shroud and the icons	39
Conclusion	44

BIBLIOGRAPHY

BAIMA BOLLONE P. L., *Sindone o no*, SEI, Turin 1993.

BALOSSINO N., *La ricerca informatica sull'immagine della Sindone,* in *Elettronica e Telecomunicazioni*, n. 1, 1996, pp. 1-11.

BALOSSINO N, TAMBURELLI G., *La datazione della Sindone e l' impronta della monetina,* in *Atti del V Congresso Nazionale di Studi sulla Sindone,* Cagliari, April 1990.

ENRIE G., *La Santa Sindone rivelata dalla fotografia*, SEI, Turin 1933.

FILAS F. L., *The identification of Pilate coins on the Shroud,* in *Sindon*, December 1983, pp. 65-73.

JACKSON J., JUMPER E. J., MOHERN B., STEVENSON K.E., *The three-dimensional image on Jesus's burial cloth,* in *Proc. U.S. Conf. Shroud of Turin.* Albuquerque, NM, March 1977, pp.74-94.

LORRE J. J. and LYNN D. J., *Digital enhancement of images of the Shroud of Turin,* in *Proc. U.S. Conf. Shroud of Turin*, Albuquerque, NM, March 1977, pp. 154-181.

MORETTO G., *Sindone, la guida*, Elle Di Ci, Turin 1996.

TAMBURELLI G., *Studio della Sindone mediante il calcolatore elettronico,* in *L'Elettronica*, n. 12, vol. LXX, 1983, pp. 1135-1149.

TAMBURELLI G., BALOSSINO N., *Ulteriori sviluppi nella elaborazione elettronica del volto sindonico.* in *Atti del IV Congresso Nazionale di Studi sulla Sindone,* Syracuse, October 1987, pp. 120.

Photographic characteristics of the Shroud

An image 'in negative'

An extraordinary characteristic of the Shroud, photographically speaking, is its 'negativity'; for the imprints behave like a photographic negative (except for the blood stains which are in positive), i.e. they are dark corresponding to the areas in relief of the man's body represented on it, and light elsewhere. Figure 1 shows the Shroud image as we see it by direct observation, the frontal part being traditionally reproduced on the left. The image is thought to show a man's body covered in dark spots, which could be wounds, and blood-stains as for example the very large one apparently corresponding to the chest.

We know that if we photograph something, we get the 'photographic negative' on the film, i.e. an image that presents light and shade completely reversed, and also spatial transposition which changes right to left and vice versa. From the negative we then get photographic copies, i.e. photographs which reproduce the object as originally seen. Figure 1 is a photograph of the Shroud as seen directly by the human eye.

Characteristics of the negative

Figure 2 shows (left) a photograph of Pope Pius XI and (right) the photographic negative in which the inversion of the levels is obvious, i.e. the dark zones and light zones have been reproduced with contrary tonalities to those of the image on the left. Furthermore, the negative presents the spatial inversion by which the Pope who in

Fig. 1

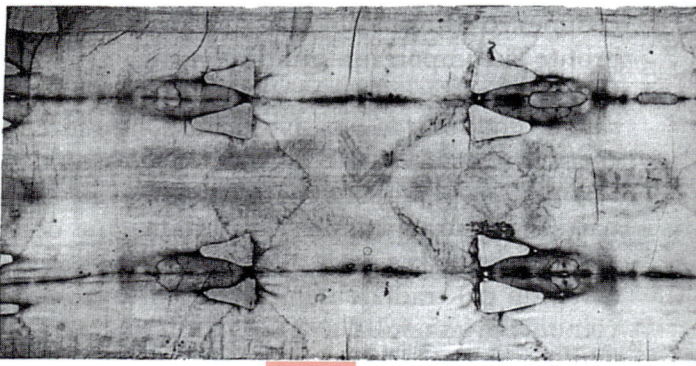

Fig. 2

positive is turning to *his* right, in the negative seems to be turning to *his* left.

We observe that the photographic negative is an image which our eyes cannot readily perceive, since it is totally different from the reality to which we are accustomed: this is in positive,

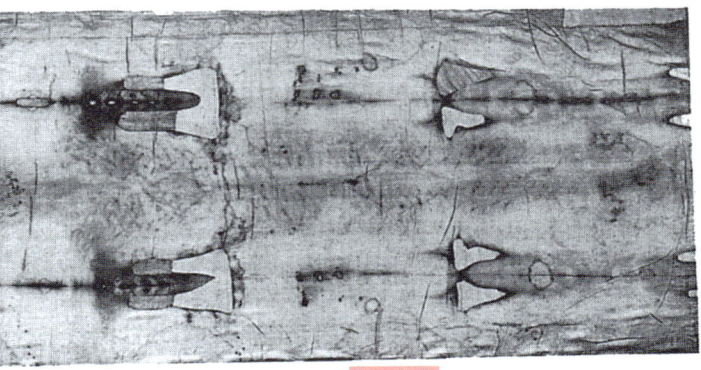

where the parts in relief or illuminated are light and those which are flat or in shadow are dark. Hence for example the cheeks of a face stand out for us and we imagine them as light, whereas the eyebrows are dark.

The 'discovery' made by S. Pia and G. Enrie

During the exposition of the Shroud in 1898, the lawyer Secondo Pia was granted permission to photograph the Shroud. When developing the negatives he saw the features of a man appear in positive (figure 3).

Later, Giuseppe Enrie's photographs taken in 1931 were to confirm the extraordinary characteristic of the imprint and stimulate research which was to diversify into many different scientific disciplines.

The photograph (figure 4) reproduces the photographic negative of the Shroud cloth, which was obtained by Enrie. It is obviously the positive figure of a man as if we could see him in front of us. This goes to support the fact that the image of the Man of the Shroud's body is a negative imprint, whereas the bloodstains are in positive.

Were the image on the Shroud a painted forgery, someone would have had to depict the figure of a man in negative. This is not at all likely, and certainly could not have been done in the Middle Ages, a period when the concept of photographic negative was as yet unknown. It was

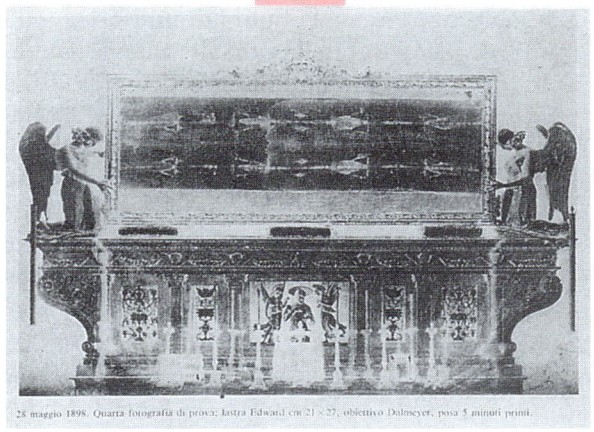

Fig. 3

to be discovered only in 1840. We observe that in the photographic negative the cloth looks completely different from that which appears to direct sight. By comparing figures 1 and 4, we note that in the negative the cloth no longer appears white but dark. On it, standing out in white, are the two parallel lines and the stains due to the fire of 1532, while the triangular patches are dark. Between the two lines you can see the figure of a man, viewed from the front and also from the back. These images, which are immediately perceptible and obvious in what they represent, show the parts of the body in relief in relation to a hypothetical plane of longitudinal symmetry running through it: thus the forehead, nose, buttocks and shoulders have light tonality, which darkens as it approaches the plane aforesaid.

A few consequences

We observe that in the photographic negative of the cloth, which presents the true appearance of the Man of the Shroud, the bleeding wounds appear light as opposed to the original image where they are in positive, i.e. dark. The wound on the left wrist, for example, and the one on the sole of the right foot appear light because they are the negative of the original image, where the blood-stains are dark, i.e. positive.

From all this it is obvious that *for a more immediate* reading of the Shroud it is better to deal with the photo *graphic negative.*

Figures 5 and 6 show the photographic positive and negative respectively of details of the face, obtained by Enrie.

If we look at the positive image of the face, we see very clearly on the left side of the forehead a blood-stain in the form of a back-to-front '3' with

Fig. 4

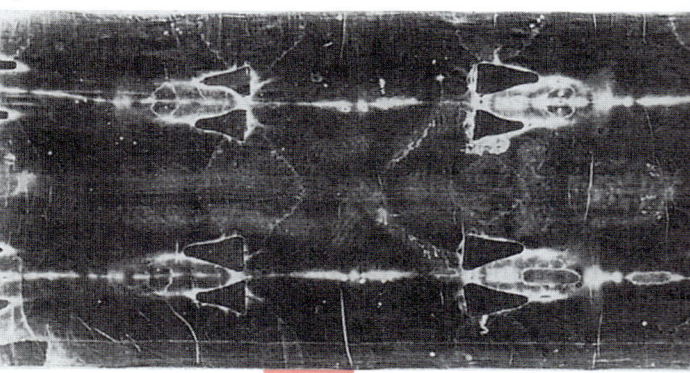

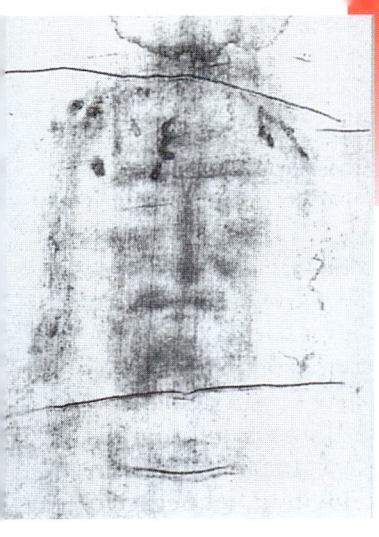

Fig. 5

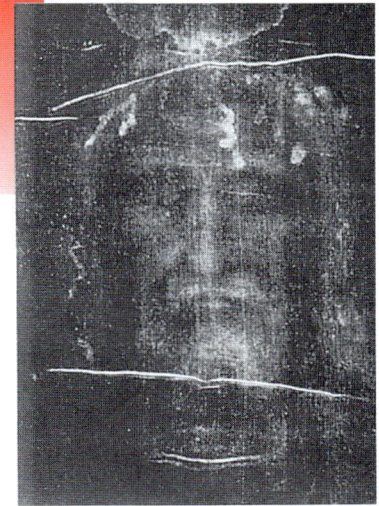

Fig. 6

dark tonality. This becomes light, in the form of a '3', on the right side of the forehead in the photographic negative. The photographic positive allows us to glimpse the lineaments of a face but does not make them intelligible. In the photographic negative however the features of a human face become clear to read.

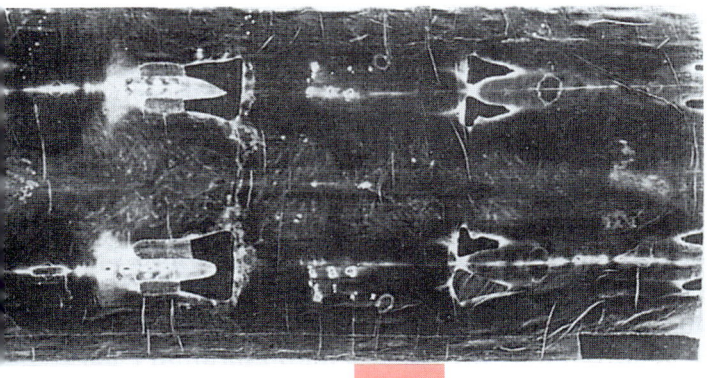

Enhancement of the Shroud with information technology

Eidomatics

Information technology can make fundamental contributions to scientific research on the Shroud. *Eidomatics* in particular (a contraction of *eides* = image and information), i.e. that area of information sciences concerned with methods for enhancing images by computer, proceeds along two lines of interest: enhancing the eidetic informational content in the Shroud so as to compare this with the gospel description, and the singling out of particular characteristics of the image so as to help show that this imprint on the cloth is not something handmade but the sign left by the corpse of a man who has suffered martyrdom.

Eidomatic methodologies

As basic premise, eidetics requires that images be translated into digital form, that is to say, as two-dimensional matrices of luminous points (*pixels*).

The number of pixels in the horizontal and vertical directions determines the 'spatial resolution', that is, the degree of detail with which the content of an image is represented. The width of the interval of variability of the luminous intensity on the other hand characterises the 'quantisation' of the luminosity, that is to say, the number of levels of grey (if we are dealing with monochrome images) contained between black and white which contribute to realising the sense of continuity between the details present in an image. Both parameters hence influence the fidelity with which the original image is reconstructed. Typical values, used in international scientific research, envisage matrices with resolution 512 x 512 pixels and 256 grey scale layers. These values have been used in enhancing the Shroud image, allowing it to be reproduced on video with a precision comparable to that of photographic processes.

Starting from the digital images, we can apply particular 'algorithms of enhancement' to show the presence, if any, of eidetic contents. In the Shroud's case digital enhancement has made it possible to obtain new *two*-dimensional and *three*-dimensional images with extremely high definition, in which details can be picked out that

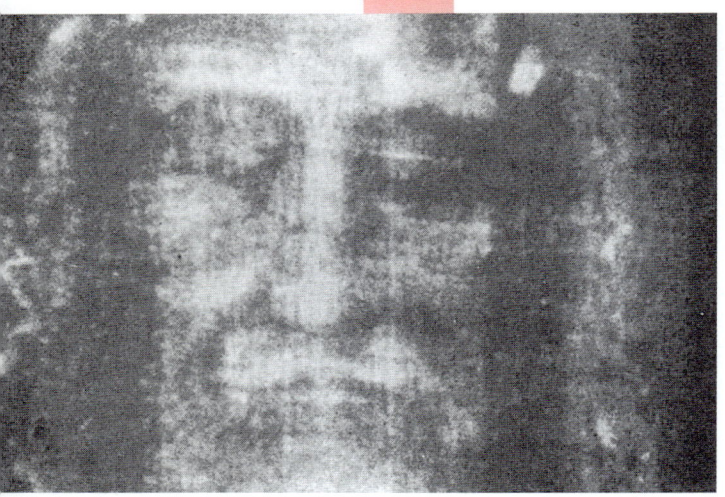

Fig. 7

cannot be seen in the original image, and most of which tally with the description given in the Gospels. The point to be made is that eidomatic methods allow us to extract whatever information is present in the original image (though this may not be immediately visible to the human eye) without introducing any artificial element.

Enhancements and filters

The purpose of eidomatic enhancements is to make the information contained in images more accessible to the human eye. They are based on the application of techniques either of scaling the levels of grey which modify contrast (i.e. the maximum variation of luminance) with a consequent increased capacity for discerning details, or of filters enhancing the luminance of a pixel on the basis of the values assumed per pixel of a surrounding area, by exploiting the correlation between them. For the human eye can perceive differences in luminance associated with the details when these differ by a value linked to the sensitivity to contrast which characterises the eye's response.

Enhancement filters are however generally used to eliminate 'noise' distorting or masking the informative content of an image, or to heighten the transitions of luminance corresponding to the contours of the structures present in the image. In the Shroud's case, disturbances of the image due to the structure and to the vicissitudes undergone by the cloth are clearly visible in figure 6 in the form of spots and isolated stains of limited dimensions. To eliminate them a filter of median type is used, and this analyses the pixels at the centre of a square window and substitutes their luminance value if this is not consistent with the presumed trend of the small area under consideration. Figure 7 shows the application of a median filter to figure 6: the spotty 'noise' has disappeared with resultant greater clarity of the image.

'Fourier's transformation'

An investigatory eidomatic instrument providing significant results in the study of the Shroud is 'Fourier's transformation' that is, a particular mathematical process which analyses a given image in terms of elementary images of sinusoidal trend of any width, frequency and orientation required, permitting its successive reconstruction. In simplified terms, 'Fourier's transformation' consists in determining, for every image, a collection of basic images which when superimposed on each other yields the image you began with.

Fig. 8

With 'Fourier's transformation' it also becomes possible to find out if, in the image, there is any favoured directionality associable with very precise structures like direction of the weave, hatching or brush-strokes.

In the case of the Shroud, if the imprint on it were a painted artifact, 'Fourier's transformation' would show it is a painting from the typically favoured directionality of the brush-strokes. Figure 8 represents 'Fourier's transformation' of the face in figure 6, showing there are no preferred directions – the latter would show up as little clusters of luminous points scattered round a central one. It is therefore clear that the Shroud image has not been made by a painter.

Three-dimensionality

Studies by two U.S. scientists

Computer study of the Shroud began in 1977 with the two Americans, Eric J. Jumper and John P. Jackson who, by information technology, plotted a further extraordinary characteristic of the image, not present in ordinary photographs or in any drawing or painting: three-dimensionality.

Three-dimensionality is the characteristic of a body to extend in three directions. An image presents three-dimensional characteristics if it is possible to extract the spatial information of the body that it represents. Three-dimensionality is shown by luminance values which vary in function of the distance of the parts of the body itself with respect to a plane of reference, which in the Shroud's case coincides with the cloth. The brown-coloured tones present on the Shroud image are very marked for the more prominent parts of the figure, i.e. forehead, nose, chest and chin, but vanish for the others: between tonality of light, therefore, and relief there must be a very definite mathematical relationship.

The first person to note that the intensity of the Shroud image seemed to vary inversely with the distance between linen and body – i.e. the nearer the body is to the sheet, the darker the image appears – was the French biologist Paul Vignon in 1902, a period when it was impossible to test the hypothesis put forward for lack of automatic enhancing devices. For their three-dimensional enhancement, the American research scientists were to adopt a hyperbolic law for converting the intensity of the pixels of the image into a finite value for relief, obtaining the three-dimensional image of the body and face.

The Turin research team and its discoveries

After attending a conference on the Shroud in May 1978, Professor Giovanni Tamburelli of the University of Turin was still dissatisfied with the quality of the images of the body and especially of the face obtained by Jumper and Jackson. These presented less definition than the original two-dimensional image, i.e. they did not permit the reading of any extra details than were already visible on the two-dimensional image. Tamburelli then formed a research team in Turin, to initiate information technology studies on the Shroud. First results were obtained as early as summer 1978 and in the following years were constantly being up-dated and amplified. These studies are still going ahead in the Department of Information Technology (even after Tamburelli's death which occurred in 1990), co-ordinated by the author of the present booklet.

In digital three-dimensional enhancement, it is postulated that the sheet either had an adequate curvature and, that is to say, that it assumed the form of a regular curved surface with a definite slope between the nose and forehead, or that it was in contact with those parts of the body of maximum luminous intensity.

The distance between the body and the cloth is evaluated according to the vertical line, given that the body is lying on its back. The hypothesis advanced is that all the points of a region surrounding the point of direct correspondence with the pixel of the image have contributed to the formation of that pixel of the image.

The law of transformation adopted is based on a serial development in which the coefficients have been appropriately varied in such a way as to obtain maximum definition of the images. The laws used for the face and the body are however

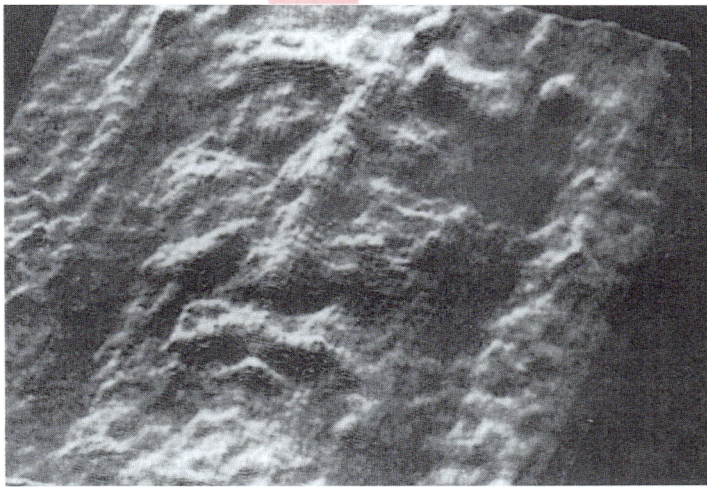

Fig. 9

not the same, since the distribution of blood obviously differs in the two cases.

To produce the three-dimensional enhancements, the team set out with appropriately filtered images, which however showed marked contrast and hence also had a high value of signal/disturbance relationship.

The result of enhancement for the face is reproduced in figure 9 where surprisingly an all-over regular relief and a somewhat heightened definition appear.

Figure 10 by way of contrast reproduces the front part of the body. The results obtained fully confirm the three-dimensional origin of the Shroud image: the relief and definition of the

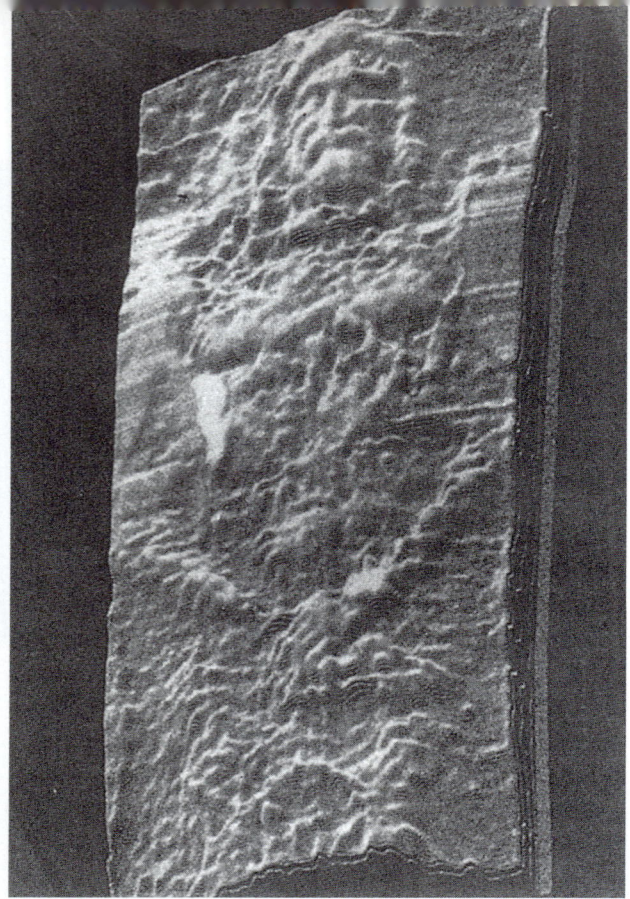

Fig. 10

various details are impressive whether humanly or scientifically speaking.

The two eidomatic enhancements of the face and body are very important because they have allowed us to pick out many details and features which in the originally two-dimensional images cannot be checked, or only doubtfully so.

With the help of the data provided by eidomatic enhancement we can indeed read on the sheet virtually all the tortures endured by the Man of the Shroud – tortures which through observation show themselves in all respects to be comparable to those endured by Jesus Christ and described in the Gospels.

The fact that some details have emerged only after three-dimensional enhancement rules out the possibility of there having been some sort of manual interference in the forming of the Shroud image. For it is inconceivable that important details, invisible to the naked eye and visible only after enhancement, could have been inserted by artifice on the image.

Detailed analysis of the three-dimensional image

Facts emerging from this research

Referring to figure 11 which reproduces the image of the face with the main characteristics indicated and numbered from 1 to 20, we can now list the facts that have emerged from eidomatic research in conjunction with what has already been found on the two-dimensional images and has thus now been definitely confirmed, linking them to the most likely hypotheses for interpreting them.

The data which image enhancement has produced on the face of the Man of the Shroud are as follows:

Foyles Bookshop
113-119 Charing Cross Rd
London WC2H 0EB

Tel: 020 7437 5660
And now at Waterloo & the Royal
Nat'l Theatre, Westfield Stratford City

VAT No:
Tel: 020

13   Terminal10

Thanks   VA

Books   30.00 Z
Books
Books   30.00 Z
Cash
Books   30.00 Z

SUBTOTAL   29.48

TOTAL   29.48
CASH   30.00
CHANGE   0.52

If you are not happy with your purchase
simply return it in a resaleable
condition with your receipt within a
month. We will refund your money
or arrange an exchange.

Foyles Bookshop
Ba Scerj Charing Cross Rd
113-119 Charing Cross Rd
London WC2H 0EB

Tel: 020 7437 5660
VAT No: 230 4004 11

Item [Avilsei] Price all in Detail NO
Acadenic descriptor price Qty
Tel: 020 7437 5660

VAT No: 230 4004 11
Tel: 020 7437 5660

2 offsetted Item 15 times Total 90.40 TT

AV   ATD
Product   T

Hends-on UI appne
IBF65C59048   1   2.05 Z
Confessions
INTIPOTIOSM   1   2.66 Z
Love the little
IBF80ETT09IS   1   2.66 Z

87.62   SF.82   ZERO RATE Z

TOTAL   28.82
CASH   30.00
TENDERED TOTAL   30.00
CHANGE   0.2

If you are not happy with your purchase
Simply return it in its original
condition with your receipt within 14
days of purchase for an exchange or
refund.

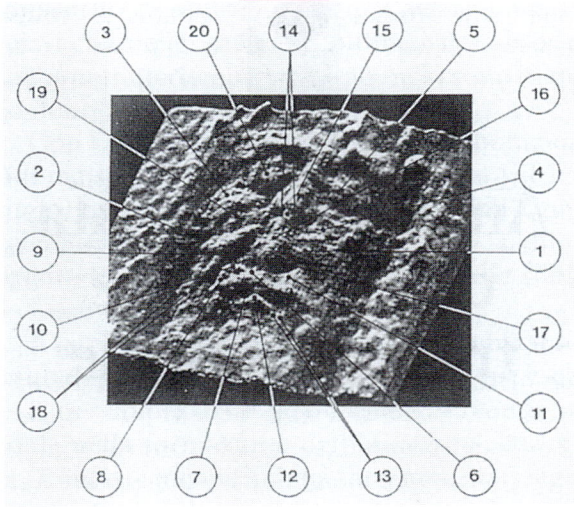

Fig. 11

— blood present on the entire face probably due to haematohydrosis, i.e.. the sweating of blood;
— the trickles and clots of blood generally flowing towards the front of the face and hair, a fact confirming that the Man of the Shroud died on the cross;
— the blood clot present on the left cheek near the nostril (1), marking a cut probably caused by something pointed;
— the track beginning on the right side of the hair, running lightly across the right cheek and over the nose to end at the blood clot just men-

tioned (2); this seems very probably to indicate that the pointed object – see (1) above – had originally been propped against the right-hand side of the hair and had then slid across, producing the cut and blood clot;

– the swelling on the right cheekbone (3)

– the cuts on the left cheekbone (4) due to contusions probably caused by blows or by falling on uneven ground; corresponding to these injuries, the spikes of the cap-of-thorns have embedded themselves in the skin on the left-hand side of the forehead, giving rise to the trickle of blood down the left side of the face and also other trickles that have soaked into the hair;

– the streaky blood clot on the left eyelid (5) due to blood flowing from the forehead where it has been cut by the spikes of the cap-of-thorns;

– the two trickles of blood coming out of the nose (6);

– the bead of blood under the upper lip (7);

– the drop of blood on the left side of the upper lip (8), showing the angle of inclination of the head immediately after death;

– the pointed drop of blood on the right nostril (9), corresponding to a gradual reflux of blood when the head was lying back, i.e. after death;

– the blood clot on the right side of the upper lip (10);

– the blood clot on the left side of the upper lip (11);

– the blood clot on the lower lip, below the

drop of blood falling from the central part of the upper lip (12);

– the steeply falling shape of the two trickles of blood on the left side of the lower lip (13);

– the two holes positioned sideways to the nose (14), perhaps conforming in shape and size to wounds caused by the tips of a Roman scourge;

– the broken nose, due to blows (15);

– the swelling at the end of the nose (16)

– the slight deflection of the end of the nose (17);

– the drops of blood on the right side of the beard (18);

– the furrow on the right cheek, corresponding to the mark left by some bruising object (19);

– the circular imprint on the right eyelid (20), probably caused by a coin used to keep the corpse's eyelid closed.

The Shroud's natural face

'Cleaning' the face

Many wounds appear on the three-dimensional image of the face, marring its beauty. They also make the face look as though it belongs to a man who is not particularly young. For people who think the man was Jesus of Nazareth, this comes as a surprise since historians think Jesus was only between 35 and 37 when he was put to death.

Nonetheless, the heightened definition of the three-dimensional image of the face allows us to catch a glimpse of the natural features of the Man of the Shroud. It is therefore of great interest to tackle the problem of cleaning the three-dimensional face of its wounds and blood-marks, so as to obtain a face as near as possible to the natural one, i.e. to what the man looked like before undergoing the tortures described in the Gospels, in a word, before his passion.

By applying appropriate filters, the signs of torture have been eliminated without distorting the underlying features. The image thus obtained is shown in figure 12, where the features appear very distinctly. This is the only *three*-dimensional image as yet obtained of the face of the Man of

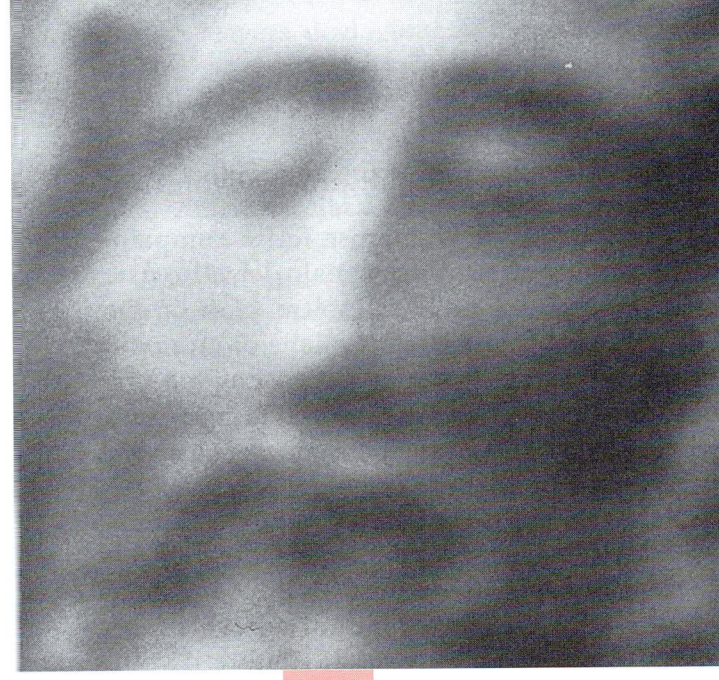

Fig. 12

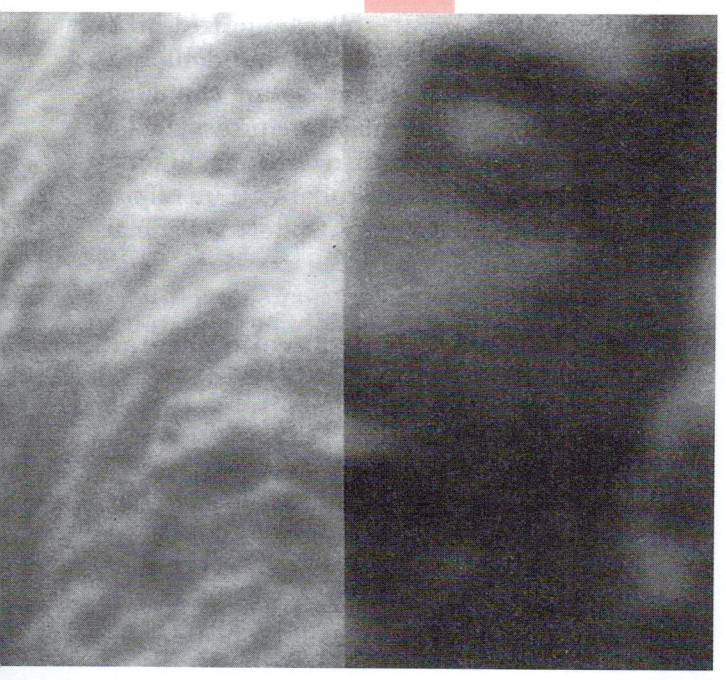

Fig. 13

the Shroud. Note: the sight fuzziness of the image is proof that the enhancement achieved is the result of digital filtering, which has a hazy look as a side-effect. Nothing however has been introduced artificially.

An image very close to the Man of the Shroud's natural face

We must emphasise that the information contained in figure 12 is exclusively what is present in the original Shroud image, cleaned of the content due to injuries. For the enhancements achieved have not introduced any additional information. It must therefore be regarded as being very close to the true image of the Man of the Shroud's face before he underwent torture and crucifixion. The remaining differences are probably due to a general tumefaction of the face and to *rigor mortis*.

Figure 13 shows how the filtering has maintained the three-dimensional aspect, and how the traumata due to the wounds can still be seen. If the Man of the Shroud had been old, filtering would not have been able to eliminate the wrinkles caused by old age. The objection is thus exploded that the Man of the Shroud could not be Jesus Christ because the two-dimensional and three-dimensional images of the face with its wounds look like those of an aged man.

Imprints of coins in the hollows of the eyes

Small coins on the eyes

Analysis of imprints in relief in the orbital zones of the Shroud face which can be related to forms of Roman coins are of the greatest importance for dating the Shroud. For proof of the existence of coin imprints on the Shroud image would provide final confirmation of the Shroud's authenticity and would also date it on internal evidence. It is obviously very unlikely that a counterfeiter of the Middle Ages would have introduced so detailed a piece of information, not immediately visible to the naked eye and associated with a custom unknown in his own epoch.

Identifying the coins

Research into the presence of coin imprints in the hollows of the Man of the Shroud's eyes was begun in 1951 by the Chicago theologian F. L. Filas, who carried out a series of studies in the photographic and numismatic fields. Starting from a copy of the original photographic plate of the Shroud, dating from 1931 and made by G. Enrie, Father Filas claimed, on the Shroud face's right eyelid, to have detected imprints very like those on the reverse of a coin, a *dilepton lituus*, which displays on the right the symbol of the *lituus*, i.e. a kind of shepherd's crook, surrounded by the Greek inscription ΤΙΒΕΡΙΟΥ ΚΑΙΣΑΡΟΣ. Such a coin, dating from the time of Tiberius as we gather from the date on the obverse of the coin, weighs little more than one gram and has a diameter of about 15mm. Specimens have been discovered showing deformations of the coins themselves and variations in the inscriptions.

In some specimens the inscription ΤΙΒΕΡΙΟΥ CAICAROS is clearly to be seen, where the Greek letter K is replaced by the Latin letter C, pronounced the same, while the letter Σ also easily becomes a C (crescent-shaped *sigma*).

The best view of the coin imprint is obtained by looking at the photographic negative of the cloth life-size or slightly enlarged as is shown in figure 14.

A shape recalling the shape of the *lituus* is

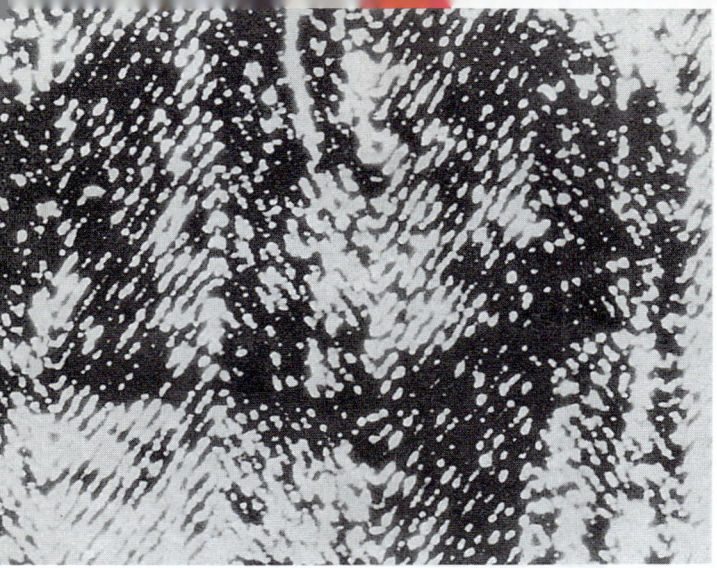

Fig. 14

recognisable, surrounded by the letter Y, which may be the last letter of the word TIBEPIOY, separated from the letters CAI forming part of the word CAISAROS or CAICAPOC.

When we subject the detail on the photographic negative of the imprint on the right eyelid to three-dimensional enhancement, we get the result seen in figure 15.

Checking out what the coin is

As we can see, an astrologer's staff can be glimpsed, shaped like a question mark, and round the upper left edge structures associable with the letter Y, separated from the letter C, followed by the letters A and I. Since three-dimensional enhancement of the photographic negative throws a shape like a back-to-front astrologer's staff in relief, we can deduce that the coin must have shown a question mark. For by placing a coin with a question mark symbol on the face, an astrologer's staff is formed by transference on the cloth, and this would once again appear as a question mark on the photographic negative. It follows from this that we must postulate the existence of a coin with the astrologer's staff in mirror-reversal of the one postulated by Father Filas.

Verification that a coin of the period exists bearing on the reverse a staff shaped like a question mark we owe to the numismatist Mario Moroni, who possesses some of them (figure 16). What we have here is a *dilepton lituus* of back-to-front type, issued by Pontius Pilate in the sixteenth year of Tiberius's reign. Its presence on the right eyelid allows the Shroud to be dated unequivocally.

Fig. 16

The sixteenth year of Tiberius...

The presence of a coin on the left eyelid was considered at the same time as the one on the right. From observation of the two-dimensional and three-dimensional images however, no shape appears that could relate to the imprint of a coin.

Observation of the arch of the eyebrows however shows, in the three-dimensional image, a curious protuberance, which suggests it may be due to a foreign body. Enhancement of the two-dimensional image of this area allowed the present author and Prof. Baima Bollone to demonstrate the presence of signs identifiable with a *lepton simpulum*. In particular, from observation of the two-dimensional image (figure 17) shapes were glimpsed of a structure calling to mind a cup,

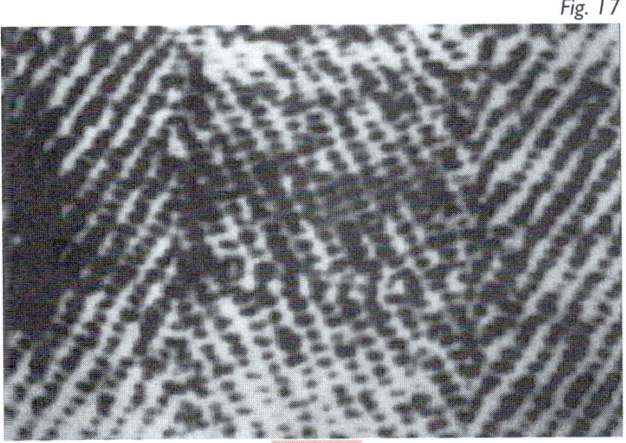

Fig. 17

Fig. 18

and three letters which can be read as LIS. Numismatic experts know that these three letters mean 'sixteenth year', where L stands for year, I for 10 and S for 6. So we are talking of year XVI of the Emperor Tiberius, which corresponds to the year 29 of the Christian era. This is the date when the coin was minted, a *lepton simpulum* (figure 18) of which there are numerous examples showing the device of a ritual cup, i.e. a *simpulum*. This coin circulated in Jewish markets and was given in small change. As well as the simpulum in the centre, the coin bore the inscription ΤΙΒΕΡΙΟΥ ΚΑΙΣΑΡΟΣ with the final initials LIS giving the date.

The Shroud
and the icons

The heightened definition of the three-dimensional image allows us to recapture the natural face of the Man of the Shroud (figure 12). From an eidomatic point of view, this result allows us to check what degree of correspondence, supported by historico-iconographical research, there may be between the Man of the Shroud's face and the more important of the icons depicting the face of Christ.

To make the comparison in the most direct way a direct, frontal representation of the face in figure 12 had to be achieved by means of three-dimensional rotation. The result of the enhancement is shown in figure 19.

Some of the best known and most important icons of Christ, starting from the sixth century, were then digitised, so as to make a comparative analysis with the three-dimensional image of the Man of the Shroud, direct and with wounds removed; they are:
– Christ of the Mandylion (sixth century);
– Christ of the church of Santa Sophia, Salonika (seventh century);
– Christ Pantocrator, Daphni (eleventh century);
– Christ blessing, Monreale Cathedral (twelfth century);
– Christ of the Meliore Toscano (thirteenth century);
– Christ of the Chilandari Monastery (thirteenth century).

Fig. 19

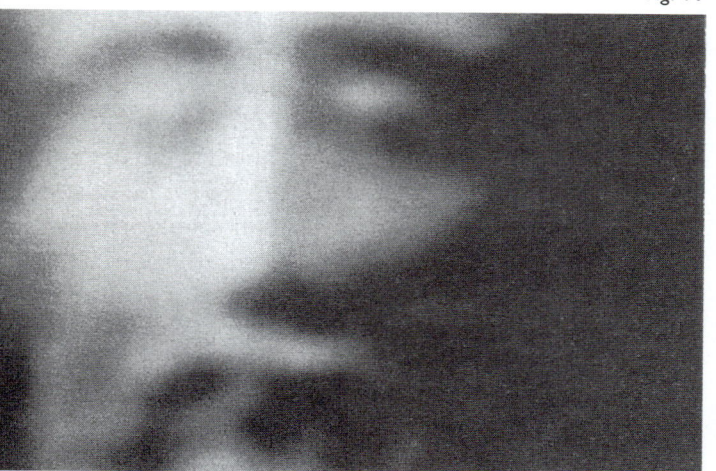

Fig. 20

Figure 20 shows four of the above-mentioned icons: top left, Christ of the Mandylion; top right, Christ Pantocrator; bottom left, Christ blessing, and bottom right, Christ of the Chilandari Monastery.

Comparison by superimposing the contours of the various faces of Christ represented in these icons – contours obtained with a translational algorithm – reveals the existence of features common to them all and confirms that a single and constant image of Christ has been handed down through the centuries (figure 21).

The next step has been to superimpose the characteristic facial features of the said icons on

Fig.21

Fig.22

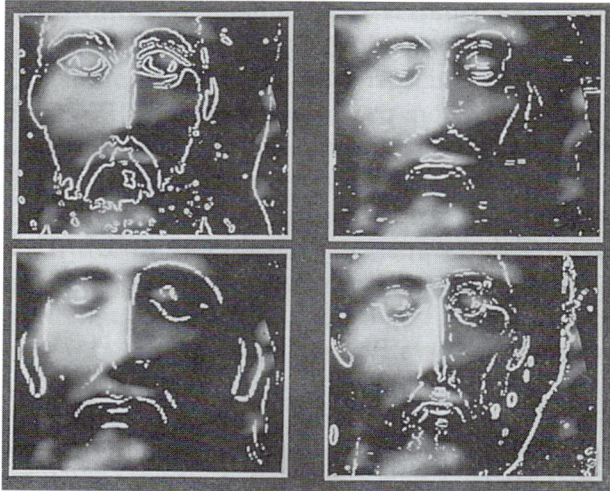

the three-dimensional image of the Man of the Shroud, direct and with wounds expunged. In figure 22, we reproduce as an example the face of the Man of the Shroud with the contours of the icons in figure 20 superimposed on it.

The results obtained show so very high a number of points of congruence as to make the hypothesis that the Man of the Shroud's face was the prototype inspiring Christian iconography at least from the sixth century onwards a very tenable one.

Conclusion

Eidomatics has furnished indispensable contributions to establishing the authenticity of the Shroud. In particular, it is only by means of instruments of information technology have we been able to reveal an internal and most important aspect of the Shroud's image: its *three-dimensionality*.

The fact that the image on the cloth is not the product of painting emerges from the application of 'Fourier's transformation' a mathematical technique developed in the eighteenth century but only of practical use since the advent of modern computers.

Only by means of digital filters is it possible

to clean images corrupted by 'noise' without introducing artificial elements. The natural face of the Man of the Shroud is hence an expression of the potential of information technology instruments. Furthermore, the use of eidomatics has made it possible to interpret imprints and be able to identify them with images stamped on Roman coins, and also easily to compare them with characteristic structures extracted from the faces of Christian iconography.